Outside the Box
Mind Mapping Your Financial Plan

By Jurgen Rudolph

Copyright © 2014 Jurgen Rudolph
All rights reserved.
ISBN-10: 1500647799
ISBN-13: 978-1500647797

What's Inside...

- 5   **Introduction**
- 7   **Acknowledgements**
- 9   **Outside the Box!**
- 12   **Why Don't More People Have a Strategic Plan in Place?**
- 14   **What Do People Need to Understand about Doing Their Financial Plan?**
- 18   **How Does the Painless Financial Plan Work?**
- 22   **The Outside the Box Process Works for Everyone**
- 24   **What Are the Mistakes People Make with Their Financial Planning?**
- 25   **Here's How to Get Started Mind Mapping Your Financial Plan**
- 26   **Here's How to Get Your Financial Mind Map Documented and Designed in Just 30 Minutes**
- 27   **About the Author**

Introduction

Outside the Box
August 2014

Do you find yourself wondering if you have enough resources for the future?

Do you need help overcoming the procrastination around planning your finances?

Clueless about how to build your own plan?

You will learn how to plan your finances yourself with confidence.

For decades we have used the same format for planning: sentences that are structured left to right on the page and from top to bottom, add a graph and some future values charts and that is more or less the structure.

As we evolve, the need for personalizing and understanding a financial plan increases. I have found through personal research using a mind map visual with people's input on their assets and plans, that a visual plan is more engaging than a traditional linear plan. Not only more engaging, but I have found there is more understanding of the plan than before which leads to shorter meetings.

Learn the basic 5 circles for your plan and grow from there; discover a way in which you can keep track of your progress.

I wrote this book to share with you the process which has helped the people I invest for and has led to better decision making and planning about their future.

I hope you enjoy the book and that the ideas presented get you thinking about your bigger future.

To Your Success!

Jurgen Rudolph

Acknowledgements

The Mind Map process evolved in the background over, approximately, the last 10 years. And I need to thank some people who knowingly or unknowingly helped with their ideas:

To Ian for introducing me to mind map and using a different approach for capturing our plans and ideas.

To you, most likely if you are reading this you were part of the development of this process. What I mean by that is even though this is a book available to all, my intent as I put it together is to have a tool for the 30 people I focus on planning for. If you are shocked to be in this group you may also be in the cool 50 or so pro bono people I also work for.

And the beautiful country and people of Costa Rica. My twice a year trips to escape to the warm Pacific waters and allow my creative side to work. Cultures other than our own I believe can only add to our creative side.

A special note to the intro: Costa Rica for many years led the world in deforestation, mainly so the people could earn a living. This has changed now and there is awareness of the importance of our natural resources.

All of the proceeds from this book go towards planting more trees; as a result, Books for Trees. On my numerous trips to Costa Rica, I became friends with a family and ended up purchasing a small parcel of land in the mountains. Half of it had been cleared years ago for pasture and crops. I have started a small replanting program, and like anything, I am learning along the way. The goal of this book is education of an evolved way to plan your finances, however by putting the proceeds of the book back into trees I believe it is also contributing to sustainability education.

Outside the Box!

Susan: Good afternoon. This is Susan Austin and I'm excited to be here with Jurgen Rudolph from Hamilton, Ontario. We are going to be discussing your new idea for making your financial planning painless and fun. Welcome, Jurgen.

Jurgen: Thank you, Susan. Glad to be here.

Susan: What do you mean by Outside the Box Jurgen?

Jurgen: I have been a financial planner for 25 years. I have purchased and sampled a number of financial planning programs. The financial planning programs that I have used over those 25 years have all been similar. The problems I would come across in meetings with people would be it's a generic program or set up for most people, not being adaptable to all situations, confusing and data intensive, just to name a few problems.

So my idea was to come up with a way to limit or cut down the amount of words we had in our financial plans. Actually it was an enlightening moment for me, about a year ago, a very simple financial planning software program was brought into my office and I was going through it to try it out and the people who were showing me how it works had left, and while it all made sense while they were here, as soon as they left, I started working on it by myself and my assistant could hear me cursing away up in my office.

It was frustrating because I had to fit people that have unique situations into a rigid planning program. We're all individuals. Everyone's situation is different is what I found during my years of financial planning. So I sat there and tried to figure out a better way. I thought why not use the mind map process and have you, the person, as the hub and create a visual so someone can see at a glance where they were financially? I wanted to eliminate all these endless words in the financial plan and be able to get it down to one page where you could actually visualize where you are today but also see at a glance where you needed to go next.

Susan: These financial plans are normally how many pages long?

Jurgen: It depends on the plan, however, on average, I would say it is 3 to 4 pages; all words and no pictures.

Susan: Having a whole bunch of words on the page doesn't really draw us a picture does it?

Jurgen: Interestingly, when I started out as a financial planner it was with a large insurance company that had a focus on training. This company had a retirement program that is still popular today it was a very successful marketing process of financial planning for retirement, and the process was using a flip chart, and that engaged the person into this flip chart that went through a binder of questions and on the pages you recorded what you wanted for your future. But over the years, everything went digitized and we sort of lost that engagement with the flip chart and moved on to power point presentations. So

I thought maybe we can bring the engagement back. I do this process on a whiteboard in my office. What I do is I draw this series of circles, or baskets, and the person is in the middle. Because of technology however, we can now capture the whiteboard on a picture and store it for future use.

Susan: Very good. Is this financial plan something you do just once?

Jurgen: Oh, great question. That's part of why you want to do it. I think you should be taking a look at your financial health quarterly. Or at least twice a year. The reason people don't do it more often and don't do it on a regular basis is because it's very hard to sit down and do your balance sheet, your income statement, make some notes and adjustments to your financial plan. I don't see that happening a lot now. People are too busy nowadays and for the most part have little time for planning.

The power of being able to do this process quickly, and often, is the growth and understanding you receive from doing it.

Why Don't More People Have a Strategic Plan in Place?

Susan: We never stop and sit down and do this sort of strategic planning. Why do you think that is? Why do you think people don't sit down and plan for their future more often?

Jurgen: Everything seems to be moving so fast in our world right now. We don't really take the time to appreciate what we've already accomplished to date and the simple approach to this system allows you to do that. You capture the information once - simply, you are drawing a mind map picture versus writing out your financial plan.

Susan: Right, so you can see at a glance where you're improving. What do you think gets in the way of people taking the time to work on this sort of strategic financial plan? Why aren't we doing this more often?

Jurgen: I have an example from today using the Outside the Box for someone that was solving a problem of the proper amount of insurance they needed. It was fairly complicated. There were support issues for children. There was a business, and this is a process that would have taken me a couple of hours to deliver a plan previously, but with the Outside the Box system I was able to do it in half an hour on a whiteboard.

Susan: Oh, wow. Okay.

Jurgen: I was then able to take a picture of it and show this individual and he just got it, just like that. It's really very simple. You could do this process yourself, and you are the architect of your own plan.

What Do People Need to Understand about Doing their Financial Plan?

Susan: Very good. What does someone who wants to use these need to understand?

Jurgen: It's pretty straight forward. We would start off with drawing circles. In Canada, you would draw a circle for your pension, one for your insurance, one for your home, another circle for what I call an open or tax account and one for tax-free savings accounts. There are five circles. You could also draw this on a piece of paper. I however use a whiteboard as, for me, it is easy to edit.

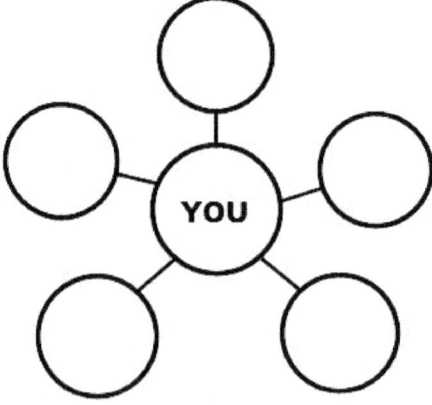

Outside The Box
Your Finanical Plan Mind Map

Susan: Right, so five circles.

Jurgen: The convenience of this is it can be expanded depending on the person and their situation, but to start, you just need those five circles.

I believe in the US you wouldn't have a tax-free savings account, and also your pension (RSP) would be called a 401(k).

Susan: Correct.

Jurgen: Insurance, can be identified using the circles. For example one circle for insurance savings, and one for term, those circles themselves can now be expanded out to other secondary circles to expand upon the primary one, in Canada, an individual's pension could also have what's called a locked-in pension because the person has left a job and they still get their commuted pension value from their job which is very common nowadays, and also their 401(k) which up here is known as an RSP, therefore, you can have separate baskets branching off from the one named pension.

You can view this all on one page, and you've drawn it up yourself.

Susan: The goal here is, after completing this exercise, we'll have a one-page snapshot of our whole financial health?

Jurgen: Yes, exactly. I am finding more and more uses for the mind mapping system. For example, as a Balance Sheet; you use your Home Value Minus Mortgage for the Net Amount; Pension Savings with accumulated balances; Leverage Account Balances, showing the Net Balance. A plan to add assets later can be shown, some actual examples that I have experienced in meetings are: Rental Property, Tax-Free Savings, Operating and Holding Companies.

The picture can be used as an Income Statement, so you know the deposits/premiums going to each area of your plan or map.

Susan: Right. You can see at a glance if maybe one area is out of balance?

Jurgen: Yes. The ability to see an area that is out of balance I think will help lead to better financial decision making. It helps avoid hiding an underdeveloped area of your plan.

Susan: This is something that they would sit down and do a kind of revisit, as you said, four times a year at a minimum to see how the numbers are shifting and changing.

Jurgen: Yes, to see how the numbers are changing is important. We've made it easy and fun for people to see at a glance where things are. No more dreading the visit to the financial planner. It's the ability for you to be able to make the most informed decisions with your money, and you are able to picture it and have a strategy. The majority of the circles, or baskets, contain assets that later in your life you will be using for an income.

Susan: Yeah, I would think that it would be kind of cool to look back and see where you were a couple of years ago versus now.

Jurgen: Having a history, of your plans, I believe is important as I find it helps for future planning. I love the Mark Twain quote, "history doesn't repeat, but it does rhyme". Having a one page picture of your financial plan is easier to review and store mentally and digitally than the traditional financial plan of many pages.

How Does the Painless Financial Plan Work?

Susan: Walk us through this as far as the five circles. You know, you put your name in the middle and you've got these five circles around you with the basic items, home, pension, tax, insurance and savings. What do you do next?

Jurgen: Yes, once you have the basic picture you may want to expand on the circles to add more details to that area. The insurance area is a great example as someone may have critical illness insurance, term insurance and also savings insurance. This can all be shown in individual micro circles that spoke off from the main insurance circle.

The Open or Tax Account can also show a leverage account and a savings account, these also spoke off of the main circle, being this time the Open or Tax circle.

Susan: So if you were missing that insurance, would that show up using this process?

Jurgen: Yes, often I will draw attention to that area by using a highlighter also, mention it is for future planning or is missing from their plan.

Susan: Okay, good.

Jurgen: I also want to mention you can also show different people, such as a couple. The insurance area is a good example as there may be different amounts of insurance per person. This can be shown in the picture by adding a circle to show what is specific to that person.

Susan: What about one of the other circles?

Jurgen: Other circles not mentioned are Pension which could contain in Canada circles for Registered Savings Plan (RSP), Spousal RSP, Locked-In Retirement Account (LIRA). Using the sub circles, you are able to draw all this under the Pension Circle.

The Tax Free Savings (TFSA) circle I find is evolving in Canada as it has been around for only 6 years. A strategy I find helpful with the TFSA is being able to use sub circles to show both people's holdings in a couple situation.

The last circle is the Home. I like to use this in the Financial Plan. In the beginning you may track it as a "Market Value minus Mortgage equals Equity" Asset, however, later the home can be a paid off asset that may be used as leverage for future assets.

I like to mention my situation. I purchased a small building to have my office in. At the time there were holes in the wall and, actually, it was a Power of Sale. I was unable to get a loan from the bank, however this was not a problem as I had equity with my home. I knew over the long term I could turn a low-valued asset such as this Power of Sale building into a valuable asset. So, I like the home "circle" as a focus for planning.

A couple of other circles that are used in specific situations are Holding Companies and also Registered Education Savings Plans for children.

Susan: Then the RESP that is your retirement plan?

Jurgen: RSP is Retirement Savings Plan and RESP is a Registered Education Savings Plan. In Canada we receive a grant for savings for your child's university or college education.

Susan: Right, and then you can see once you reach a certain amount that you think is fair or when you get to the amount then you know that that circle is sort of complete.

Jurgen: Yes, you can view it all as a picture. The amounts are all in front of you to see what is complete.

Susan: If you were targeting this book in the United States you'd have to have a circle for debt to show how much debt someone has. Credit card debt, student loan debt, auto loans etc.

Jurgen: Yes, that can be bad debt or non-deductible debt.

Susan: Right, you almost don't want them on your plan, but if they have debt I'd think you'd want to figure out a way to get rid of them as part of your plan?

Jurgen: Yes, you can add a circle to the plan that is named non-deductible debt. And out of that circle you can branch to the different areas that have the debt. However, I must disclose that I have not used that yet. As Outside the Box evolves I will have more to share on showing the non-deductible debt.

Susan: Very good.

Jurgen: This debt circle can be used to form a strategy to be "debt free".

Susan: Americans are big on our cars here and paying cash isn't always an option. How do you see what someone's net worth is, are they able to do that easily from this?

Jurgen: Yes because your net worth is your assets minus your liabilities. Using the Outside the Box process you are able to build a picture of your net worth. You can then see the areas you may want to add to or concentrate on.

Susan: Very good.

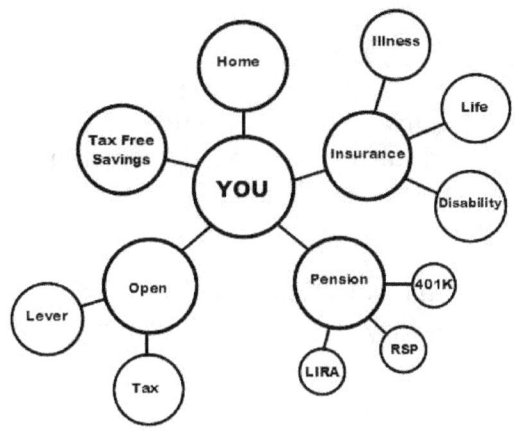

Outside The Box
Your Finanical Plan Mind Map

The Outside the Box Process Works for Everyone

Susan: Have you found anyone this wouldn't work for?

Jurgen: No, not yet.

Susan: Yeah, okay I can see that. What is some of the feedback you've gotten from the clients you've used this with? What are the clients' responses to having this process?

Jurgen: I'm smiling as you ask that question. A great example comes to mind.

Kim, who works with me, has her office on the main floor. I prepare the picture and do the meetings on the second floor. This particular case was a friend who, while he was leaving after a meeting, on the way out of the office said to Kim, "that was painless."

Susan: Painless, because?

Jurgen: I think he was expecting the plan to be traditional and full of many details as assumptions. Instead it was an engaging personalized picture of his situation financially.

Susan: When you make that appointment with them, what do they think they're coming in to have done?

Jurgen: I tell them, if it's the first time, that I will be drawing them a picture on a whiteboard. Most times I will also say, that it is worth the investment in time to come to the office, as opposed to me travelling to them.

The picture, the visual itself, engages the couple or the person in the process, they're helping solve it, and also they are the centre of the plan. It makes it very personal. It gives them the power to understand their own financial plan.

Susan: Because normally with financial planning, it's a little intimidating...

Jurgen: Yes, it can be. I find with this process though you are not in over your head.

Susan: Because the circles are all parts that relate directly to their life. There's nothing on the whiteboard, or in the plan, that doesn't relate right to the person? You're not talking about some abstract thing here, you're talking about how it can affect their lives and as you said their bigger future?

Jurgen: Yes, it's an original plan designed to their unique situation and it's drawn right in front of them. Also, you can do it yourself, if you want to.

What Are the Mistakes People Make with Their Financial Planning?

Susan: Are there any mistakes? Could you mess this up?

Jurgen: I think the errors that can be made would be misstating a value.

Susan: If someone is not saving enough, it's all right here. You can't keep your head in the sand. You know what I mean? If they don't have the right protection or if they're not saving for retirement at the level that they should be, it's right here on paper. There's no denying it, right?

Jurgen: Yeah. Well, you don't have to do it. You also don't have to eat healthy, I guess. This is just if you want to do it, here's a way.

Susan: Very true. This is just great Jurgen. I can see the value in being able to see your whole life from a financial point of view being laid out so simply and as your client said, so painlessly. This should be taught in schools you know?

Jurgen: Well thanks. I can't take all the credit it's been an exciting process to use with everyone I work with. It's a tool to get them to see, at a glance, the future they are working on building. So we are super excited to be using this with people to help them forecast and build their wealth.

Here's How to Get Started Mind Mapping Your Financial Plan

Susan: Thanks Jurgen. If someone has questions, how can they reach you?

Jurgen: They can e-mail me at: info@jkrfinancial.com and I'd be glad to help.

Here's How to Get Your Financial Mind Map Documented and Designed in Just 30 Minutes

You already know that planning for your future is important. The confusing part is not knowing how to create a cohesive yet evolving financial plan in just minutes.

That's where we come in. We help people just like you map out their financial future in an easy to read and understand format like you've never seen before.

Step 1: We invest 30 minutes capturing your current financial snapshot.

Step 2: We then show you how to use this mind map to build the financial wellness you need.

Step 3: We take it from there and work with you to improve on your current financial status.

Most people think it takes hours of hard work trying to document their financial plan. Now you can create your financial road map in just 30 minutes.

If you'd like us to help, just send an email to: info@jkrfinancial.com and we will take it from there.

About the Author

Born and raised in Hamilton, Ontario, Jurgen is the oldest of 5 boys. He lived in England for 2 years for early high school. After high school he joined the Canadian military (PPCLI) and was stationed in Germany for 4 years. Jurgen has 25 years experience as a Financial Planner with London Life & MSIL/CMG. Jurgen is an avid outdoors man and currently has a brown belt in Brazilian Jiu Jitsu and considers this a lifetime pursuit of excellence.

Every year Jurgen spends a month in Costa Rica surfing and enjoying relaxing and rejuvenating. Jurgen is passionate about helping others have the life of their dreams. When he's not working Jurgen loves spending his time with his 5 year old daughter.

Outside The Box
Your Finanical Plan Mind Map

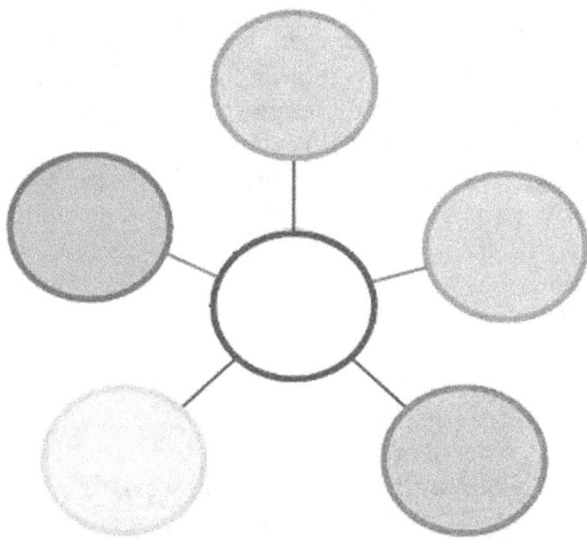

Notes

Notes

Notes

Notes

Notes

Notes

Notes

Notes

Notes

Notes

www.ingramcontent.com/pod-product-compliance
Lightning Source LLC
Chambersburg PA
CBHW072045190526
45165CB00018B/1825